Behind the Eyes of Juvenile Delinquents

Rev. Billy J. Strawter, Sr.

APu
Author Promotions Unlimited, Inc.
A-P-U Publishing Group

Copyright © 1999 by EnviCare Consulting, Inc.

All rights reserved. No part of this book may be reproduced or transmitted in any form or by any means, electronic or mechanical, including photocopying, recording, or by any informational storage or retrieval system, without written permission from the publisher.

Actual names of all youngsters mentioned or referred to in this book have been changed for protection of privacy.

Scriptures quotation from the HOLY BIBLE, NEW INTERNATIONAL VERSION. Copyright © 1973, 1978, 1984 by International Bible Society. Used by permission of Zondervan Publishing House.

To contact the author, write to:
Reverend Billy J. Strawter, Sr.
EnviCare Consulting, Inc.
2809 Blairmount Drive
Midland, MI 48642
(p) 517-839-9177

Publisher's mailing address:
APU Publishing Group
P.O. Box 1137, Edgewood, MD 21040
(P) 410-538-7400 (F) 410-538-7468
Email: apupb@mciworld.com

Library of Congress Catalog Card Number: 99-76107

Strawter, Sr., Billy J.
Behind the Eyes of Juvenile Delinquents
    1. Juveniles 2. Criminal justice system 3. Youth, in America 4. Self-help/Self-help development for youth 5. Inspiration/motivation for youth

ISBN: 1-878647-66-0

5-4-3-2

To my wife, Lee Anna Strawter, for her editorial help, her words of encouragement and constructive criticism, and to the young people in the Saginaw County Juvenile Detention Center.

Acknowledgments

First, my greatest thanks goes to God for giving me the time and strength to write this book.

I thank my children, B.J. and Kilah, for sharing their enthusiasm with me as I wrote this book; and, I'm grateful to all the youth in the Saginaw County Juvenile Detention Center for their participation.

I give thanks to my sisters and brother, Debbie, Shirley, and Ronnie for their support and love. I give special thanks to my father and mother, O.Z. and Mary Strawter, for bringing me into this world and for their love.

I appreciate Ann Holmon, Nikita Murray, Pennye Padgett and Rev. Joseph Mortensen for their editorial assistance.

Special thanks goes to the staffs of the Saginaw Juvenile Detention Center for support and their work at the facility. Thanks to Chris Hinton, Virginia Padilla, Mike Gerard, Larry Gordon, Dan Wressell, Bob Sawyer, Tim Metro and Judge Faye Harrison for their support. Thanks to all the volunteers, Rev. Eddie Benson, David Vercellino, Blaine Williams, and Jim Schmeider who assisted me on Tuesdays at the Detention Center and to Donna Shipman for working with the girls on Thursday evenings. Thanks to the Tri-County Youth for Christ for filling in the gap to implement the Youth Guidance Ministry at the Detention Center and to Tabernacle Baptist Church for their services.

Contents

Introduction — 8

Chapter 1: ***Touching the Hearts of Young People*** — 11

Chapter 2: ***An Adventure With Young People*** — 15
  The Beginning — 15
  Called by God — 15
  Building Trust — 17
  Dealing With Different Attitudes — 19
  Responding to Negative Behavior — 22
  Dealing With Personal Confrontation — 23
  Why Reach Out to Youth? — 24
  Building a Relationship With Youth — 25
  Words of Encouragement — 26
  Principles of Success — 26

Chapter 3: ***How Juvenile Delinquents End Up in Trouble*** — 30
  Good Homes — 31
  The Reason I Did It — 32

Chapter 4: ***Anger Has Control Over Young People*** — 41
  What Makes Young People Angry? — 41
  Disciplining Young People — 45

Chapter 5: ***Profiles of Troubled Young People*** — 48
  The Role of the Father — 50
  Experiencing the Pains of Life — 53
  Wishing for Something Better — 56

Chapter 6: *Stopping the Destruction of Young People* 67
   What Is Destroying Our Young People? 67
   A Mother's Live-in Boyfriend Impacts a Youth's Life 74
   What Are the Solutions for Juvenile Delinquents? 76
   Who Can Make a Difference in a Troubled
      Youth's Life? 77

Chapter 7: *My Perspective of Young People* 91

Epilogue 96

About the Author 100

Introduction

This book was first written for people interested in working and witnessing to youngsters in trouble. It was also prepared for people who enjoy inspirational reading; people who are moved by God to support programs designed to work with troubled youth; parents who want to rear their youngsters to be positive, productive members of society; parents who want to turn their youngsters away from their destructive behavior; and, young people who need assistance getting on the right track. This book is designed to speak to a diverse group of readers.

This book deals with rebellious children's feelings, experiences and emotions that led them to make wrong choices. It also focuses on prevention and redemption to help potential parents to rear their youngsters by giving an inspiring story of youngsters in a juvenile detention center whose sad, broken lives get turned around when they come to Christ. After reading this book, my greatest hope is that parents and young people will learn from others' mistakes so they will not travel down that same broad road that leads to destruction.

Enter through the narrow gate. For wide is the gate and broad is the road that leads to destruction, and many enter through it. But small is the gate and narrow the road that leads to life, and only a few find it. Matthew 7:13-14.

This book deals with the reasons why young people:
- Make certain decisions,
- Feel so much hopelessness,
- Feel they cannot change,
- Are involved with drugs,
- Feel no one cares about them,
- Continue to do the same self-defeating things over and over,
- Run away from home,
- Become involved with gangs,
- Do not like to attend school,
- Become pregnant at an early age,
- Think fighting will solve their conflicts,
- Have promiscuous sex,
- Do not attend church,
- Do not like to apply for jobs,
- Feel as they do about their parent(s),
- Feel their lives would have turned out differently if they grew up in a home with both a mother and a father,
- Get angry.

This information comes from my direct experiences working with young people over the past several years in a Detention Center, and from society in general. It is not based on statistical data. Rather, it is about what young people have shared with me. Although I do not profess to have all the answers to young people's problems, I do believe that you can learn from my experiences with youth which will enhance your ability to make a difference in the lives of young people.

Lastly, I have also written about myself to show how God prepared me for ministry in the hope that adults will be encouraged to get involved in mentoring troubled youth. God inspired me to share with you my thoughts and experiences with young people. I hope each reader will be blessed by God and will choose to open their hearts to troubled young people and their parents or guardians. I believe we have a responsibility as believers of Jesus Christ to lift the spirit of young people from the bondage of low self-esteem, drugs, alcohol, gang involvement, deception, and robbery by reaching out to them and not just by prayer or mere words.

What good is it, my brother, if a man claims to have faith but has no deeds? Can such faith save him? Suppose a brother or sister is without clothes and daily food; if one of you says to him, "Go, I wish you well; keep warm and well fed." But does nothing about his physical needs what good is it? In the same way, faith by itself, if not accompanied by action, is dead. James 2:14-17.

Rev. Billy J. Strawter, Sr.

ONE

Touching the Hearts of Young People

I had an opportunity to visit Jeffery, Duke, Robert, Parker, and Jamal in their unit at the Saginaw County Juvenile Detention Center to read from my manuscript, *Behind the Eyes of Juvenile Delinquents*. When I arrived in the unit, Jeffery, Duke and Jamal were playing cards. Robert and Parker were watching the movie "Spawn" on television. I sat beside them just to inquire about their activities for the day. Each shared that they had a good day. But they were still interested in watching television and playing cards. I told them that I had come by the unit to read from the manuscript as promised.

Jeffery, Duke and Jamal slowly stopped playing cards and Robert stopped watching television and they all came to listen to the story as I read. Then Jeffery, Duke, Jamal and Robert became angry with Parker because he continued to watch television. They told me Parker worshiped Satan. I asked the other boys to leave him alone because Parker was serving his master. I said, "You tell me you love God but yet you are not serving him. If you were serving Him, more than likely you would not be in the Detention Center. I wish you were as faithful to God as Parker was to his master. You are in worse condition than Parker because you know the truth and refuse to live by the truth."

After I spoke those words, everyone calmed down. I continued to read from the manuscript to Jeffery, Duke, Jamal and Robert. They were captivated by the words being read because they knew it was about them as well as myself. They stored it all into their minds as they sat and listened intently.

It's difficult to describe what I felt, but what struck me most was the reaction of Parker who, during all this time, had his back turned to us. He got out of his chair and went behind us to lie on top of the ping pong table which was near us. A glance from the corner of my left eye showed that we now had Parker's attention. Parker asked, "Where did you get that information from?"

I told Parker I got the information from the youth in the Detention Center.

Robert said, "He wrote it himself," as if he was proud of me.

Parker continued to lie on the table as I read from the manuscript. As we continued, to my surprise, Parker got a chair and sat right in front of us. He listened intently as I continued to read with a smile on my face, because I was glad we had his attention which gave me hope that I was exerting a positive impact on his life. Before I knew it, time had expired.

As I was leaving the unit, Parker told me that he didn't serve Satan but was trying to determine the right way to go.

I told him I understood and hoped he would start going to church. Then Parker told me he was going to attend church in the Detention Center. He also wanted to know when was I going to read the rest of the manuscript to them. I told him I probably would not because of other activities scheduled.

Well, I looked for Parker on the following Tuesday evening but he did not show up. I told the others to tell Parker I inquired about him. They told me he stayed back in the unit to watch television.

Sunday of the following week, Parker showed up in church. I was elated to see him. I never considered that the words I read would have such an impact on Parker's life, but one should never be surprised about the operation of the Holy Spirit. If no one else is impacted by this book, I will always cherish the words spoken by Parker when he said that he was trying to determine the right direction and that he would attend church in the Detention Center. I hope he will make the correct choices. I did not force my beliefs on him or try to debate with him about his beliefs. Parker said he was rebelling against his parents and that he grew up in the church. I hope he will turn his life over to Jesus Christ.

Parker's response encouraged me to continue my work with rebellious adolescents. You never know what words or actions will stop the destructive behavior of a young person when God uses you as a vehicle.

Please pray that God will change the hearts of troubled youths and their parents and/or guardians so that they will call upon the Lord for divine wisdom, knowledge and understanding. In doing so, young people's parents and/or guardians will have more success with their youngster.

The second chapter will deal specifically with the Lord preparing me for my involvement with young people at the Civitan (Saginaw local community center) and the Saginaw County Juvenile Detention Center, both located in Saginaw, Michigan. The ministry at the Detention Center and the Civitan was coordinated by Tri-County Youth for Christ.

TWO

An Adventure With Young People

The Beginning

I was blessed to become one of the founders of Tri-County Youth for Christ and its chairman of the board. I also served as a volunteer in the campus life ministry to lead small youth groups in the inner city for three years at the Civitan in Saginaw. During the ministry at the Civitan, I learned more about the behavior of adolescents and their needs during those three years I coordinated the program. The volunteers who shared their time and talents blessed the young people with their testimonies and time.

Called by God

In 1991, the Saginaw County Juvenile Detention Center had an opening for a staff minister. At that time, I was board Chairman for Tri-County Youth for Christ and was leading the Campus Life group at the Civitan center along with Ruby. Ruby volunteered her time with the Tri-County Youth for Christ. She had a caring heart and understood troubled youth. Ruby and I had built some valuable relationships with the young people.

When I left the Civitan, I was concerned about being accepted by the young people in the Detention Center and about the availability of study materials needed to reach out to juvenile delinquents. Nevertheless, the Lord granted me wisdom to generate various topics for discussion. My responsibility was to lead group discussions and provide counseling. Sunday morning worship services were held at 8:45 a.m., in the Gym of the Detention Center. It started early enough for me to be present at Faith Ministries Baptist Church by 10:00 a.m., since I was the associate minister. My pastor supported my absence from Sunday school to conduct services at the Detention Center. Approximately forty-two beds were available for both boys and girls when I started at the Detention Center. They have added fifteen beds to the facility.

Approximately sixty percent of the youth would attend Tuesday's and Sunday's meetings. I was alone and without any volunteers to assist me at the time. My first Tuesday night meeting with the young people was very uncomfortable. Their eyes seemed to pierce through me similar to x-rays used to identify broken bones in the human body. They were checking me out to see if I was serious about reaching out to them.

Initially, I started with prayer and warm-up games

to get the youth relaxed and comfortable with me. The first meeting went well. The executive director of Tri-County Youth for Christ was at the first meeting. Over a period of time, the Lord led me to discontinue the games and instead to feed the young people with His Word. When I did just what the Spirit led me to do, the meetings continued to progress well. The Lord revealed to me the importance of focusing on His Word. I was astonished at how well they accepted the change.

Our God is a mighty God who anoints His people to perform His will, when we accept and trust His divine guidance.

Building Trust

I had to learn how to trust the Lord every time I went to the Detention Center because I knew I was fighting a spiritual battle and needed God's protection.

"Finally, be strong in the Lord and in his mighty power. Put on the full armor of God so that you can take your stand against the devil's schemes. For our struggle is not against flesh and blood, but against the rulers, against the authority, against the powers of this dark world and against the spiritual forces of evil in the heavenly realms." - Ephesians 6:10-11.

The young people were still checking me out. They had no desire to open their hearts to a stranger. They observed me from head to toe—my clothing, my hair, my expressions and my choice of words. It required constant work for me, as well as the young people to build respect and trust for one another. They came to church in the Detention Center on a voluntary basis. Some came to the meetings just to get out of their living area. There were some who wanted to use me to get out of the Detention Center. In most situations, the Lord revealed to me those individuals who were trying to take advantage of the situation. Some really came to seek God and wanted to change. Over half attended Tuesday and Sunday events. It took about two to four weeks for me to gain their trust.

When I was away from the Detention Center for two weeks or more, I had to work hard again to rebuild trust. When new youngsters came, I had problems until we reached a point of understanding and they became familiar with the Detention Center's rules.

Trust was very important to the young people. They desired to know I was committed to what I said and did. In other words, my actions spoke louder than my words. Trust was gained by my listening to their point of view regardless of how crazy it sounded. Trust was earned and maintained by being committed to loving them just the way they were, yet hoping for a positive change in their life. They trusted me because I listened, hugged and shook their hands and I never confronted them in front of their peers. I would firmly let them know when they were wrong without condemning them.

Dealing With Different Attitudes

The most difficult part of ministering to trouble youth was learning to deal with the different attitudes of the young people and the attitudes of some of the staff workers. Some of the workers were there just to receive a paycheck. Others really cared about making a difference in the lives of young adults.

When I arrived at the Detention Center one Tuesday around 6:45 p.m., I was glad to be there to share scripture and words of encouragement with the youth. As they came to the gymnasium, they all seemed happy. Suddenly I saw a staff member send Paul, a juvenile detainee, back to his room. Then I saw Joseph becoming angry because of what had happened to Paul. Joseph felt that staff personnel had made the wrong decision. So I intervened by walking over to Joseph and putting my arms around him. I asked, "What's the problem?"

He said, "It didn't make any sense that staff was sending Paul back. He was just asking him a question."

I said, with my arm still around him, "I understand you are upset but you will be sent back to the room too if you don't calm down."

Joseph kept saying it didn't make any sense and he was furious. With my arm on his shoulder, I asked him, "Do you remember what I said about controlling your attitude and temper?"

He said, "Yes," and calmed down. If I had responded

negatively, it would have caused Joseph to be more agitated. Sometimes all a young person needs is a compassionate ear and someone to validate their feelings. A touch of love and commitment toward the interest of the troubled youth can work miracles.

Dealing with youth staring at each other in the units was a concern because of the use of gang signs. The boys enjoyed looking at the girls and rival gang members stared and gave gang signs that were forbidden inside the Detention Center. However, the center's staff did an excellent job of controlling potential gang activity by reinforcing the use of consequences of using gang signs. I never knew whether behavior problems that occurred in the youth's living quarters were affecting the youth guidance ministry meetings. When a problem occurs in the unit, it's sometimes difficult to keep the youngsters focused.

I had to keep my eyes focused on the youth to ensure they were not going to cause a problem in the meeting. The young people were separated into three units (Unit A, B & C). Unit C only consisted of girls. Subsequent to each meeting, it was necessary for me to explain my four simple rules of conduct to minimize any misunderstandings between the youth and myself. I wasn't sure how they would respond to the rules of conduct listed below:

- Please do not talk while I am speaking.

- If you have something to say I will acknowledge you but it must be decent and in order.
- You are in the house of the Lord; please treat it with respect.
- If I see you talking, I will ask if you have something to share so do not think I am trying to confront you.

They accepted the rules and acknowledged me as their spiritual leader. Thanks to God for their acceptance.

I remember during one Thursday night meeting with the youngsters, Dan walked out of the counseling session because he did not want to hear the Word of God. He was in the Detention Center for assault. He was blind to the truth—the truth based on God's Word. I was afraid I had missed an opportunity to influence his life since I had not tactfully used the right words. I had to release the fear of worrying about using the right words. My duty was to teach them the Word of God. Eventually, Dan returned a week later and to my surprise, he apologized. He said, "I'm sorry about walking out of the meeting."

The Lord confirmed I had communicated the truth to Dan and that he had received it. I realized that I could not let the fear of rejection keep me from doing God's will.

In order to meet the needs of a person like Dan, I

had to maintain a balanced relationship between my family and ministry for the Lord. I had two teenagers at the time and a full-time job at the Dow Chemical Company and a marriage that was very important to me. I knew my own house had to be in order or it would be very difficult to reach people like Dan or anyone else.

The support from my spouse, son and daughter made it easier to reach out to the youth at the Detention Center and other areas of ministry. I am thankful that God gave my family the wisdom to understand the work I was doing. They made my ministry possible by their love, support and encouragement.

"He must manage his own family well and see that his children obey him with proper respect. If anyone does not know how to manage his own family, how can he take care of God's church?" Timothy 3: 4-5.

Responding to Negative Behavior

The most effective way I handled negative behavior of youngsters was to calm them down and help them to reflect on the potential consequences of their actions. This type of response usually worked well because behind their eyes (in their minds), they knew I was more concerned about them than myself. I usually didn't experience problems with youngsters until the staff overreacted to their negative behavior during our meetings.

When negative behavior occurred among youngsters during a small group discussions where I had a good relationship with a core group, the youths would confront disruptive persons for being disrespectful. I would respond to them by saying, "Let me handle this please," and smiled without anger. I knew they respected me and did not want anyone to be disrespectful towards me.

Dealing With Personal Confrontation

I avoided personal confrontation with youngsters in the Detention Center as if it were a deadly plague used by Satan to fuel a spiritual battle that only God can win because I could not win in the flesh. I immediately covered the fuel of confrontation with showers of Jesus Christ's love and understanding. I asked staff to become involved only if it was necessary. The youth had to be removed if they refused to listened to staff or had the potential to harm someone.

I had only one detainee removed from service in seven years of volunteering at the Detention Center. I knew the individual would have had a negative affect on the small group discussion. I tried to avoid removing someone at all costs because it could deepen the problems of the individual if not handled properly. Often, young people are searching for real love, unconditional love, but they are searching in all the wrong places. Those involved in gangs often believe their gang members care more for them than their own family. When they end up in trouble, unfortunately, they find out that gang members only offered a temporary love.

Why Reach Out to Youth?

I have learned that adults should avoid reaching out to rebellious youth simply because they feel youngsters have a need. A person must be called by the Lord to have the greatest influence on troubled young persons' lives with genuine concern. Fervent prayer and love is essential to reach the heart of troubled youth because they are influenced by evil.

"Finally, be strong in the Lord and in his mighty power. Put on the full armor of God so that you can take your stand against the devil's schemes. For our struggle is not against flesh and blood, but against the rulers, against the authorities, against the powers of this dark world and against the spiritual forces of evil in the heavenly realms." Ephesians 6:10-12.

These young people are like a locomotive out of control until something stops them. They need mentors who can understand and relate to them. Their mentors should be the parents and siblings. They need to be shown the true meaning of unconditional love and taught how to return love unconditionally. We need to help them put away their self-destructive ways and give them hope in order to carry on with their life in a positive and productive manner. They need to know how to serve the Lord with joy and understand they are accountable for their own actions. They typically blame others in life for the wrong they have performed such as their friends, family and society.

We need to encourage these young people to control their attitude and temper because of how it affects their behavior in a negative way. They need to learn how to deal with the environment they live in and how to positively influence the condition of their neighborhood. If they can destroy their neighborhood with gangs, drugs and crime, they definitely can build it up with goodness.

Building a Relationship With Youth

My first step in building a relationship with youth in the Detention Center was to share with them the reasons why I gave up my time to be with them. I shared with them the distance I traveled (forty miles round trip) each time to get there. Behind their eyes, it was difficult for them to understand why I committed to drive from Midland to Saginaw three times a week to be with them. I wanted them to know I was sincere in my concerns for them and my efforts to influence them in a positive way, thus willing to make a sacrifice for them.

The second step was to share my personal struggles. I shared the mistakes I had made when I was growing up. I also learned to admit to them whenever I made a mistake in the meeting. It was essential to show humility to the youngsters.

The third step was personal contact. As often as possible, I would shake their hands. Sometimes I gave them a hug and frequently said, "I love you." Sometimes I got a response and sometimes I didn't. A third ear was always listening as they shared their stories or concerns with me. My eyes stayed focused on the person speaking to let him know that his words were very important to me. After he had finished speaking, I responded, when appropriate; however, sometimes silence was the best response to prevent creating a negative situation. These youth needed to know that they were special but be made aware of the wrong choices they had made. I am amazed at how much attention they need. They really need a positive support network in their own neighborhood when they leave the Detention Center to help them stay focused on making the correct choices. Most of them complained that they lack a support system, and I agree.

Words of Encouragement

During my meetings with the young people, I have learned that constant encouragement is very important. I share with them the weaknesses and strengths I've observed in them. Often, I reinforced the fact that they could change their negative behavior. Many of the young people had tempers, which cause them to overreact. They learned to react defensively in order to protect themselves in their environment.

Principles of Success

There are three Principles of Success I encouraged youngsters to apply in their lives when they get out of the Detention Center.

Principle 1: Stay in School

I always encouraged them to stay in school by pursuing an education at a trade school, Junior college or University to obtain a degree in their area of interest. They are very intelligent and have the potential to succeed. They have many talents but need guidance to use these talents in a constructive manner. They also are advised to seek counseling at their school if they are attending one. The counselors, as well as teachers need to assist the youth to identify and develop their strengths and talents. Often, we try to direct young people into areas where they can make the most money. They will be more successful in life if we encourage them to develop the skills and talents they possess.

Principle 2: Stay Out of the Street

Young people were advised to discontinue hanging out with people who will have a negative influence on them. However, they see this as a difficult task to achieve because their home and neighborhood have not changed. For some, their siblings and parents are involved in crime and immoral acts.

In that type of situation, I encouraged them to read the Holy Bible and live according to God's Word. I reminded them that they have a choice, regardless of their circumstances. When they tried to blame others for their circumstances, I usually asked them: "Who controls your mind, body and heart?"

They usually respond, "I do."

Then I asked, "Has anyone from your neighborhood survived and gone onto college?" If their response was "yes," I asked, "Why do you think they survived the neighborhood?"

Their usual response was, "They chose to overcome their environment."

Then I would say, "You are correct. Those individuals decided they wanted more out of life than the streets and crime and you have the same opportunity."

However, often times behind their eyes, the only thing they can see is that their situation is different. They use excuses instead of admitting they have given up. They see gangs destroying their neighborhood and they see drug dealers making lots of money so they think they must do the same thing. They seek to belong, to have material "things" and get involved with undesirable criminal acts by following negative role models.

Principle 3: Go to Church

I have spoken very boldly and honestly to the young people about attending Sunday School and Sunday worship services whether their parents go or not. They are encouraged to become involved with church youth group activities and not to worry about the wrong others are doing but focus on returning to the track that leads to success. I shared with them how much God wants them to lead a joyful and happy life but they must learn to trust the Lord and obey Him.

Unfortunately, not many follow this advice once they leave the Detention Center because they lack a support network to do so.

Adults must give them hope with our services and love, but most importantly they need to learn more about God's Word. God's Word is the truth and the truth will set them free. If the Christian community fails to reach the rebellious youth someone else will reach them, and, they might not give them the truth. What the young people are searching for is love, hope, peace and stability. Most importantly, they are searching for someone who will listen intently without judgement to their broken hearts. Adults love to give advice but we have failed to listen prior to giving advice.

"We must pay more attention, therefore, to what we have heard, so that we do not drift away." Hebrew 2:1-2.

THREE

How Juvenile Delinquents End Up in Trouble

The young people in the Detention Center were asked, "Why do you love the streets?"

Their response was, "It's boring at home, and there is nothing to do!"

However, the same type of response comes from young people who are not in trouble. But, as a result of their boredom, the troubled youth seek alternatives to staying at home and doing schoolwork or house chores to aid their parents or guardians. They search for different avenues to satisfy their desires. They have confessed their desire to dress well while in school or in the streets.

Some young people will resort to stealing from their parents and eventually move on to worse crimes such as breaking and entering (B & E) or selling drugs to meet their materialistic desires and to fit into gangs. Some young people will resort to stealing to financially support their parents and they don't believe they will be caught for stealing. When they are caught, they try to figure out how to avoid getting caught the next time instead of not doing it again.

There are young people in the Detention Center who were born to teenage parents and did not receive good parental guidance. Most teenage parents do not have sufficient parental skills needed to rear a child. As a result, the child grows up not knowing how to respect others. They sometimes see themselves as an equal to their parent in many situations. Some parents treat them that way. A child must know the difference between an adult responsibility and that of a child.

The majority of the youths in the Detention Center are from single parent homes, usually live with their mother, and do not get support from their father. In some cases, the father was also involved in criminal activities, as well as other siblings in the family. Over thirty-four percent of the youths released return to the Detention Center. The percentage would be much higher if they all were caught. Parents need to become more involved with their children's physical, educational, emotional and spiritual needs. If they don't, someone else will. The family needs to become stronger by sitting down together at dinner time to share their day. The community needs to be more involved by giving support to those families that need help rearing their children.

Good Homes

There are young people in the Detention Center

that come from good homes. However, they felt their parents were too stringent and they became rebellious. Many of the girls who were in Detention Center were runaways. They were experiencing conflict with their mothers and became rebellious even though their families loved them and gave them guidance. They chose to follow the wrong crowd that led to more rebellion and conflict within the family. In situations like these, the family must maintain "tough love," and not let guilt take over, which often leads to bad attitudes and tempers flairing. It's easy to say and hard to do, but the answer is: *"Do not be overcome by evil, but overcome evil with good."* Romans 12:21.

The Reason I Did It

On Thursday nights at the Detention Center I conducted small group counseling. Here, we talked about why youngsters are involved in criminal activities such as assault, violation of placement rules, armed robbery and breaking and entering. Discussing these criminal acts gave me a better understanding of their personal characteristics, family background, and why they made certain choices.

I found that the most effective times to obtain information from youngsters were during Thursday evening's counseling sessions where they would normally open their hearts and shared freely as compared to the Tuesday evening group sessions. I spoke with them individually which allowed me to learn more about the history of their rebellious years and relationship with family members.

On one particular Thursday, I was excited about the questions planned for the youth. We were in one of the classrooms instead of the chapel. As I looked through the glass window from the classroom, I could see the sunshine in the room. Any time you see the sunshine in Michigan it brings joy because most of the time it's gray and hazy. I really felt the spirit working. When they arrived after dinner, they too were in good spirits with a willingness to share. Each person in the group shared stories of when they first started stealing, what items they took, and at what age they stole.

These are the questions, followed by some of the young people's responses.

Can you remember the first time you stole?

Tom, age seventeen, was a very good speaker and knew the right words to say. I sensed he had a good heart and needed a strong support network. He lived with his mother and father at one point but his father left the family when he was two years old. His mother was forty-three years old. The first thing Tom stole was a candy bar but he did not know at what age. When he was thirteen he graduated to stealing bikes. At age fourteen he was charged for B & E which eventually led to arm robbery.

John, age fourteen, and his mother lived with his

grandmother from the time he was an infant. His mother was thirty-one and his grandmother was sixty-five. His father left the family and he was hurt by this situation. I wished I could have taken away the hurt but the only thing I could do was listen and give my love. He stole a candy bar between the ages of seven and eight. He started breaking and entering homes at the age of fourteen.

Henry, age sixteen, lived with both parents. His mother was forty-eight and his father was fifty-two. Henry was a very bright young man. He had the desire to learn more about God. He was very likable and cared a great deal about people but he allowed the streets to control him. He stole a candy bar at the age of six and started to steal toys at age eight. He started stealing money from his relatives at the age of twelve and clothing at age fourteen. He also enjoyed stealing videotapes to sell. He was in the Detention Center for robbery. According to an adult who knew the family, Henry's parents were very strict and cared very much for him. Henry went to prison and to this day, I don't believe the court system made the correct decision because he was interested in changing his life. As an alternative, they should have sent him to boot camp.

Mike, age fifteen, lived with his mother. She was thirty-five. Mike's father was in prison. Mike stole a candy bar at the age of six. He said he had a sweet tooth. He started stealing toys around eight or nine years old. At the age of eleven he stole videotapes. At fourteen, he graduated to stealing bikes and later a car.

Greg, age fifteen, lived with his mother and with pain in his eyes, he said his father was in prison. His mother was thirty-five years old and he was fifteen. Greg had been in the Detention Center several times. It appears he was influenced by street life and his outlook was one of hopelessness. He really needed to experience the opportunity to be around a positive role model that would give "tough love." Unless God intervenes, he will continue in criminal activities. He stole candy at the age of six or seven and toys at age eight. Then he started stealing jewelry continuously. At the age twelve he started breaking and entering and stole a car.

In some cases, the parents were not aware of their children's theft habits. But there were some parents who knew their children were stealing because they hadn't purchased the extra clothing and music items their children had at home, but chose not to intervene. Tom replied eagerly, "A friend of my mother told me to tell my mother that she gave me the goods." It is inappropriate for an adult to make such a response to a child. The adult is only adding fuel to the fire.

In Henry's case, he told his mother his older sister gave him the stolen items. Apparently, the mother did not question Henry or his sister to verify the truth.

Sometime as parents, we don't want to know the truth because we are in denial or we just don't want to deal with the situation, thinking it will go away. However, that is far from the truth. It is very important to deal with this situation as soon as possible, but it must be handled with unconditional love. In other words, there should be no strings attached to the love given to the child. As a parent or guardian, we must avoid allowing our attitude and temper to control the way we discipline our youth.

Greg, with excitement, said his mother did not spare the rod but its results only lasted for a short while. John replied with sadness that his mother knew he was stealing and she only said, "You are just like your father."

Each young person is different and unique, even though they may display some of the characteristics of their parents. When a youth displays a negative characteristic of a parent, we should share strongly what is wrong with the negative behavior they are displaying and not say, "You are just like your father or mother." They might just like the negative behavior and continue it if they are not shown what is wrong with what they are doing.

Why are youths involved in gangs?

Many of the young people were very responsive to this question, and had a variety of reasons as to why they were involved in gangs. Here are some of their reasons:

1. The gang members had money and I did not.
2. Gang members went places together to beat people up.
3. Gang members "got your back" if you need protection.
4. Gangs had parties.
5. You got respect from the girls.
6. You got a lot of girls and sex.
7. Because you don't want to be a nerd.
8. My brother or cousin was in a gang.
9. You got high.
10. It was boring in my neighborhood.
11. Gangs had cars.
12. The gang was a family and if you needed something they would help you.
13. You felt as though you were somebody.
14. Drive-by shootings.

When I posed this same question to twenty-seven young people both boys and girls in 1993, the responses were the same then, as now. The reasons listed above are real to young people, even though they can lead to destruction in the long run. They do not live for the future, but for the moment. We also must encourage them to think about the future and the consequences of their negative behavior.

What type of people are involved in gangs?

They informed me that the following types of people are involved in gangs:

1. Troubled people: They viewed troubled people as young people who are experiencing problems with their parents, siblings, or guardians; young males whose mothers depend on them to be the man of the house when the father is gone; young people frustrated about finding a job.

2. Family member: Some young people got involved because someone in their family was involved in a gang and they felt the need to carry on the tradition with pride. It also creates a sense of belonging.

3. Associates: They are young people that hang out with friends who are involved in gangs.

4. Criminals: "Like attracts like," which is important for the strength of gangs. They see a common ground of despair and gravitate towards the gangs for support and a sense of family.

5. Drug dealers: When the family is suffering financially, some youth will sell drugs to supplement their family income either with or without parental knowledge.

6. Violent people: These are young people who just don't care about anything or anyone.

7. Hot heads: These are young people whose attitude and temper got the best of them.

The young people indicated that most of the time the gang members carry guns, party, get high, and are a bad influence on youth. They normally are territorial and control their turf.

What type of gang does God want?

Both boys and girls described the type of gang they thought that God would prefer. They knew the right answers but had difficulty applying God's Word to their life. Their responses are as follows.

God's gang would:
1. Help each other.
2. Become a big brother or big sister for someone else.
3. Make the neighborhood safer.
4. Develop friendships.
5. Organize neighborhood dances.
6. Help you get a job.
7. Get others to be involved in the church.
8. Work in the neighborhood to do the following:
    -Help the needy.
    -Help others.
    -Help build homes for the needy.
    -Paint houses for those in need.
    -Mow the elderlys' grass.

It would be great if all gangs could use the above as their code of operation. What a difference they could make in their neighborhoods and the world if their activities were God centered! Sometimes I wish God would anoint us with the power to zap young people to live like Jesus Christ and share their joy about Christ with others. I have ministered to over 2,000 youngsters, yet I only know a few who have learned to trust Jesus Christ with their heart, soul and mind. I hope there are many more that I just don't know about. Many of these young people want to change their lives but lack the will-power to sustain their efforts.

I remember speaking with a young man by the name of Steve. He was in the Detention Center because of an assault. He previously had other run-ins with the law for carrying a gun. Of each young person I've asked, "Why do you carry a gun?" their response was always, "I needed protection."

Steve started stealing when he was nine years old; guess what he stole? Yes, candy from a store. He said, "I seemed to always walk out of the store without paying." He lived with his mother in Saginaw, Michigan, and his father lived in Washington, D.C. He has never been involved with a gang. There are young people involved in street crime and they are not a member of a gang. So we can't blame gangs for all the crime in various neighborhoods.

FOUR

Anger Has Control Over Young People

What Makes Young People Angry?

One Tuesday evening at the Detention Center, the Lord led me to see what was behind the eyes of the youth regarding anger. I was not sure of the type of responses I would receive from the youth. However, the Lord was faithful and He really blessed us with good participation. The responses are listed below:

1. Someone talking about them behind their back.
2. When their expectations of others were not met.
3. Someone lies to them.
4. Someone disrespects them in front of others.
5. A person calling them a derogatory name (inappropriate name-calling).
6. Somebody puts their business in the street.
7. Two-faced people (tell you one thing-do something else).
8. People who always think they are right.

9. People who think they look good.
10. People who think they are more than they are.
11. People who do not keep their promise.
12. People who make you feel stupid.
13. Drive by shooting.
14. Someone breaking into your house.
15. Someone stepping on your shoes.

Since they become frustrated with the above situations, we need to teach them how to deal with those situations. We proceeded to discuss the importance of controlled anger. We discussed the need to apply Ephesians 4:26 in their life: *"In your anger do not sin: Do not let the sun go down while you are angry."*

Many young people do not easily let go of their anger. They will allow it to control them and they need to learn how to take "time out" before responding to a negative situation. I have found it very helpful to listen and talk with them about their negative behavior because it gave them something to think about and how to make other choices.

They usually tell me, "No one has ever sat down to listen and talk with us the way you do." They say, "You always listen to us and try to help us to do what is right. You don't get angry with us."

I do my very best to show love, yet be firm when they don't take responsibility for their own actions. Many of these young people are crying out for help. They have been blinded by sin and can't recognize that they really need love and hope to survive in this sinful world. They need to be taught the message behind Jeremiah 29:11: *"For I know the plans I have for you declared the Lord, plans to prosper you and not to harm you. Plans to give you hope and a future."*

I would like to share with you a letter I received from Helen crying out for help. The individual wrote this letter June 15, 1995:

Dear Rev. Strawter,

Hello! I just came back from your Bible study and it really got me to thinking. You are completely right, we should obey everyone, our parents, family, rules, instructions, most importantly, God, in which for 14 years I have not done a good job of. I mean the reason I am here is for running away (along with a ton of happenings on the side). I have been away from my home since April 23, 1995. The first time was because I received a punishment of 30 days, which I did not believe I should have gotten; so I ran-a-way from home.

I decided that running away was "fun" because I had met lots of new people that had extreme amounts of marijuana, and I could do anything I wanted until I was ready to quit. So once again I ran. After 6 or 7 attempts of running, I was still given the chance to return home.

Then one night I went home, I smelled like smoke so my mother helped me take a shower. She was right there with a towel; it was 9:00 p.m. so she made me dinner. We had a long talk, "I love you talk" then she told me she was extremely tired so I could stay up to watch TV, whatever. And she said she loved me a lot and I said the same. Ten minutes later she came back down stairs and said, "Helen, please don't run tonight, things will work out?"

I comforted her, promising her I would not. But no later than 12:30 a.m., I was gone on one more of my little adventures. This last time was June 1, 4:00 a.m. when three other guys and myself were out, stealing cars, and were caught. I went to court and they placed me in here. I really had no idea what everyone was telling me when they said, " You do not know what you are doing!" and all those other things. But, now, being in here has taken these thoughts out of hiding. I realize what being in a gang, doing drugs, running away, and so on, does to a teenager. My entire family loves me to death. I know this, but when I try to tell them how I feel and why I wanted to run, they just put more and more restrictions on me. It came down to the point where they put an alarm on my bedroom door at night so they would know if I tried to run. I wanted to have the life of a little gang-banger, which did not have any rules (I watched too much TV) so that's what I shot for. But now, it's not worth it, I know. But, please, just tell me how I can get God into my life and keep Him there? I pray but it's just because I am in here (Detention Center). When I get out I pray every once in a while. Please help me. I go to court the 22nd of June. Please write me and tell me how I could fight this; right now I feel alone and pretty much am, please.

P. S. Actions show everything, words mean nothing. That's what my mom always says.

My heart went out to Helen and I could only express God's love and share the comfort of His Word with her. Here's an example where a parent loved her daughter very much but in Helen's eyes her mother controlled her too much. And now she is crying out for help. I have not had an opportunity to see her since she left the Detention Center. I hope and pray God has put someone else in her life. A follow-up program is essential to ministry work in the Detention Center.

Disciplining Young People

As parents, we over react sometimes in punishing

our children; therefore we push them into hiding their weaknesses from us. I know as a parent that I have over reacted with my children, and this led to additional problems. We really need God's guidance in our life when disciplining our children.

"Fathers, do not exasperate your child. Instead, bring them up in the training and instruction of the Lord." Ephesian 6:4.

I pray and hope that Helen is doing well. And I hope her letter will open parent's eyes to their situations with their own children. Please pray for Helen and all of our young people.

When a youth is disciplined, it should always be based on the current negative behavior and not as a means to deal with past issues never addressed. In other words, never use disciplinary actions toward a child as a dumping ground for previous problems due to parental frustration. You don't want to add fuel to an already volatile situation. The desired outcome for disciplinary actions is to eliminate or minimize the negative behavior being displayed by a child. Each parent must evaluate the appropriate disciplinary actions for their child. What works for one child might not work for the other. Use a variety of disciplinary actions until you find the one that is appropriate for your child.

When possible, avoid the use of positive things to punish your child such as requiring them to mow the lawn, clean the house, wash the dishes, or wash the car. These are normal chores that they should be doing around the house anyway. Some parents use some of the following things to discipline their child such as, no television, no phone calls, no going out, no parties, no movie, no allowance, no friends over to the house this week, no new shoes or clothing this month or refined to the room. These types of disciplinary actions deal with the child's personal interest and not that of the entire family.

Do not lock your child in a room or closet or over-whip a child with a belt. Such actions could create physiological problems resulting in juvenile delinquency. Remember to always discipline a child with love and make sure they comprehend the reason(s) for your decision.

Discipline is a continuous and consistent process which sets boundaries for the child and shows the consequences of breaking those boundaries.

"Train a child in the way he should go, and when he is old he will not turn from it." Proverbs 22:6

FIVE

Profiles of Troubled Young People

During one session, we discussed with several youth their backgrounds. Here are their stories, and I want you to empathize with their pain and hurt.

A sixteen year old, whose name was Danny, was in the Detention Center for selling cocaine. He felt he was in the Detention Center because he was trying to make too much money, not because he was wrong for selling drugs. He had been selling drugs since age fourteen. Danny claimed he started selling cocaine by watching others. I've heard this same response many times from other young people.

Danny has one brother and a sister. His sister has a different father then he and his brother. He said his nineteen year old brother was locked up for six months and that he had not seen his father since he was fourteen years old. The first time he was caught was at age fourteen for stealing a bike.

Young people need the same father and same

mother. I wonder how many young people are having sex with their sister or brother unknowingly because too many men are producing babies with too many different women.

David, age thirteen, was in the Detention Center for stabbing his mother. He also was suspended from school for trying to stab another student. The first time he recalled getting into trouble with the law was for running away from home. He stayed away from home for two weeks because his father took him for two weeks without telling his mother. His mother and father were married but had gotten a divorce. He has two sisters with the same father and one brother with a different father.

In this situation, the father was wrong for encouraging his son not to be honest with his mother. The father should have informed the mother of David's location regardless of the father's relationship with his ex-wife. As parents, we should never give our children permission to be dishonest.

Mike, age fourteen, was in the Detention Center for violating probation. He was kicked out of school a lot. He got high on marijuana frequently. The first time he got in trouble was at the age ten for carrying a gun. He said, "I needed a gun for protection." He came to the Detention Center at age eleven and has been in and out ever since. He has four brothers and one sister. Each of the siblings has a different father. His mother and father are separated.

The reason I emphasized that some of the young people and their siblings had different fathers but the same mother was to show how it promotes instability rather than stability within the family and society. Youth involved in the Detention Center need stability. I know how difficult it was for my wife and I to raise our two children with the same parents who sometimes had different ideas and approaches to discipline. We were able to keep each other balanced and consistent. Youngsters need a constant in their lives.

The Role of the Father

A session was spent with young people discussing their feelings toward their fathers. The discussion was very interesting. Most of the young people still treasured their fathers even though they did not see them very much. However, they wished they could have a better relationship with their fathers. They felt their lives would have been better if that relationship had been closer.

Here are some of their responses to the question: **How do you feel about your father?**

Lamar was in the Detention Center for domestic violence at the age of sixteen. He lived with his mother. His girlfriend, who was the mother of his son, was talking to another guy, so he thought, and Lamar was arrested for fighting with her. Later on he realized she was telling the truth. He was fifteen years old when his girlfriend got pregnant. This is another example of how our young people let their tempers get the best of them. He shared with me how his father had recognized him as his son until he was ten years old. After age ten, his father decided to get a blood test to determine if he was really his son. He said he heard his mother tell his father that he was not the father of her child. He said he was hurt for two years after that incident. He still does not know the name of his real father. Even though Lamar says he was only hurt for two years after the incident, I felt during the discussion he was still hurting. My heart goes out to him. I do not know what it's like not knowing your father. Can you imagine how Lamar really felt after ten years of believing he was with his real father, then being told he was not? It's amazing he has the strength to go on in life.

Another young man whose name was Darryl, sixteen, was in the Detention Center for stealing a car and reckless driving. His mother and father do not live together. He has four sisters and three brothers. His mother is thirty-four years old. He does not wish to see his father because his father has not helped him. He said, "If I could start all over again I would want a father at home with me." Two of his sisters had different fathers and two brothers had the same father. Darryl also was hurting on the inside and needed support and encouragement.

Herman was in the Detention Center for attempted breaking and entering at the age of sixteen. His mother was forty-five and his father was forty years old. According to Herman, his parents had never married. He said he has not seen his father since he was nine or ten years old. He has two sisters and three brothers. He has a sister who was in prison. His siblings have different fathers. He has two brothers who are in prison; one for armed robbery and the other for dealing drugs.

The youngsters were asked:
What are your thoughts about your father? Here are their responses:

- I love my father, even though he is not home to help around the house.
- I loved my father until a year ago.
- I love my dad because my parents are together and my father has always been there for me.
- I do not like my father. My mother won't let my father see me because he gets drunk. I wish my father would stop drinking alcohol.
- I love my dad but I do not care to be around him because he wasn't there for me when I was young.
- I love my father for bringing me into this world but he has not been around me since I was six years old. I just do not have any feelings for my father.

Many young people love their father regardless of

the situations they have experienced with them. They really need to experience substaining a good relationship with their father in the home. If the father is no longer living at the residence, the father needs to maintain a consistent and loving relationship with his child.

Experiencing the Pains of Life

I asked several girls:

What situations led to your being in the Detention Center? These are their responses:

Martha was in the Detention Center for running away from home. She was age fifteen. She ran away from the foster home that she was placed in because her foster father told her to leave. So she left home. She was in foster care because she had previously been in the Detention Center for home invasion and another time for breaking and entering. She never explained to us why her foster father told her to leave. She had lived with her mother and two sisters prior to her criminal activities.

Sue was in the Detention Center for running away from home. She was thirteen. Her story was very interesting because I had previously not heard of this type of situation from a youth before. The reason she ran away from home was because of the bad experiences at home with her brothers. One day Sue said she walked into her home and her brothers wouldn't give her "space," which pressed her button beyond what could be tolerated. She explained the situation to her mother and nothing was done to correct it so anger influenced her to run away from home that night. Apparently, she needed her own space.

She had one sister and two brothers. One brother and sister had the same father and the other brother had a different father.

During one Tuesday session, several of the girls began to cry as we discussed why they were in the Detention Center. Most of the young girls that ran away from home did so because of poor relationships with their mothers. Their pain was so great that I had to hold back my tears so I could comfort them. Staff had to go and get tissue for them to wipe away their tears.

They were experiencing problems at home because they felt their mothers were too controlling. They admitted they had similar characteristics as their mothers. The moms and daughters were butting heads because they were too much alike. Sometimes, parents see their children doing the same things they did and come down too hard because they know how they suffered. In other words, parents don't want their children to do the same wrong things they did as a youth. It is commendable that parents don't want their children to suffer but sometimes parents must let their children make mistakes and be there when they fall with an ocean of love. When children are wrong, parents must take the appropriate steps to correct them, but not go overboard. I told the girls to cry and just let their feelings flow, and they did. They all wanted a better relationship with their mother. We have an obligation to help inspire youngsters when the opportunity presents itself.

As parents we must recognize that our children need "space" as well as we do.

Pam came to the Detention Center at age fifteen because she assaulted her father when he tried to confront her during a telephone incident. Apparently, she was on the telephone and her sister wanted to use the telephone. Her father made her get off so her sister could use the telephone. Pam felt that her sister always got special treatment but when it came to her they would not allow her to do what she wanted. She had one sister and four brothers. Their parents are together and all siblings had the same father and mother.

Even though both parents are in the home and administering unconditional love to their children, there are no guarantees that children won't perform juvenile delinquent acts. I believe when both parents are involved in their child's life, they will greatly minimize the potential of producing a rebellious child. God's Word tells us in Proverb 22:6, *"Train a child in the way he should go and when he is old he will not turn from it."*

Betty was also in the Detention Center for running away from home at the age of twelve. Her aunt had abused her. She didn't know who her father was. Her mother was fourteen years old when she was born. Betty's grandmother kicked her mother out of the house and adopted her.

Betty explained how her mother had difficulties but I felt she was trying to justify her own behavior through her mother's negative behavior. Her life is an example of how parents can influence their children in a negative way.

When parents display negative behavior, it is difficult for them to encourage their children to live a good life that is pleasing and acceptable to God because the children will remind parents of their own negative behavior.

Wishing for Something Better

We had a discussion on:

If you had one wish, what would it be? These are their responses:

- Do anything, any time, any place.

There are young people who will refuse to change but we must not give up hope because God did not give up on us. Perhaps there are others who can make a difference in their lives. I encourage every parent to leave a string attached to their rebellious child so you can reel them in when he or she falls to the bottom. As you know, that day will come and you should open your arm without condemnation or judgement.

- Go to heaven.

The Christian community must reach out to troubled youth so that they may have an opportunity to see Jesus face to face one day in heaven or on earth. We must not think that sport centers alone will change the hearts of troubled youth but we must use a combination of methods and remember God's way will last forever.

- Change my life.

I believe the majority of trouble youth can change. They just need God-fearing people in their lives to lead the way.

- Live to see my grandchildren.

Some of the youth don't believe they will survive their neighborhoods because of so much violence and hopelessness. They have seen so much death in their neighborhood. We must do something to make a difference in their lives and neighborhoods. If we don't, we will all suffer because of their foolishness. Innocence people's lives are being destroyed by troubled youth.

- Go back and change all I did.

Young people cannot change the destruction they have done toward others in the past. However, they can be taught how to say "I'm sorry" for the wrong they have done and ask for forgiveness from the person whom they have hurt.

- **Be back with my family.**
Many troubled youth wished they had a stable home. Some have had babies just so the child could return love to them. They don't think of the responsibilities associated with parenting but only the love they need. I recall a young lady named, Jennifer, who said, "I preferred the Juvenile Detention Center rather than home because I have it better in here." What a sad story for this child that circumstances at home are so undesirable that she preferred the Detention Center.

- **Make the future better.**
There are many talented troubled youth who can make a valuable contribution to society when put on the right track. We have an obligation to show them the right track by our good examples.

- **Be a millionaire.**
There are trouble youth that have the potential in the future to become great business leaders, doctors, educators, etc., but have not locked on to the opportunity given to them or some were not given the opportunity.

- Stay out of trouble and do better.

They can minimize the trouble they get into with the help of churches, community, businesses, Juvenile Court System, federal, state and local governments, educational institutions, foundations and volunteers.

- Go home.

They can return to home and society one day if only they listen to the advice given to them.

I told them I wished for them the following:
- Allow God to change their lives.
- Become successful.
- Get an education.
- Become doctors, lawyers, teachers, dentists, chemists, social workers, firemen, mechanics, sanitary engineers and computer technicians.
- Become good mothers and fathers in the future.
- Make a difference in other's lives and their neighborhood.
- Follow the three principles of success.

As previously mentioned, the three principles to apply toward staying out of trouble are:
-Stay in school
-Stay out of the streets, and
-Go to church

I also asked the youngsters:

What type of person do you look forward to dating?
The responses to this question were from both girls and boys:

- A person with a job, gold, car and house (Girl).
- A person that was fine (body well built) and has a car (Guy).
- A person who is smart, good, has a job, and likes me for who I am (Girl).
- A person with a house, good job and a body (Girls & Guys).
- A person with a good personality (Girls & Guys).
- A person that's not a rat (Girls & Guys).
- A person that has not been a juvenile delinquent detention (Juvie) rat (Girls & Guys).

We had fun with the above question. Twenty-seven of twenty-eight young people said they would not marry someone who had been in the Detention Center. Well, I said, "That means none of you will ever get married if people outside the Detention Center feel the same way."

This response was necessary to give them something to ponder. But most importantly, I told them that as long as the person has repented of their wrong doing from the heart, God will forgive them and they must do the same.

It was amazing that they didn't want someone like

themselves. This indicates that most of them didn't like their behavior. They have learned to accept their negative behavior as reality because of their environment. However, they must not use their environment as an excuse not to make the right choices.

The next question was:
Who do you look up to (as a role model)? I was curious to see how the youth would respond to this question. I'm sure some may have copied responses but it gives a feel as to how some youth relate to role models. Their responses are listed below:

- My brother is my role model because he got in trouble like me but he changed his life.

This youth was twelve years old and very intelligent. I had an opportunity to witness to his brother when he was in the Detention Center and he received Christ while in the Detention Center. I have not heard from his brother since he received his freedom.

- My dad is my role model because he tried to obtain custody of me but my mother would not let him. This young man had lived his life in the Detention Center, in other words, in and out of the facility frequently. He had been on drugs. He really needs a good network if he is to survive.

- I look up to myself because everyone has done something bad in life. This youngster had excellent speaking abilities but used his intelligence to try to conquer the legal system. He was in the Detention Center for breaking into a house. He broke into the house because he was drunk and then got caught when he fell asleep.

He also used drugs. He has the potential to become an excellent lawyer, and I encouraged him to pursue becoming one.

- My family (Grandparents). Some young people recognize the importance of family and the need for a stable home. They wish one day their lives would become better.

Young people have different kinds of role models. These role models may have a lasting impression on the hearts of our young people. They need to see families that are united together in love and reaching out to improve their undeveloped communities.

Another question was:
What do you want people to see behind your eyes (in your mind)?

- Good sense of humor: Each young person is unique in his own way. They can have a good sense of humor if they would allow the beautiful roses inside of them to bloom like flowers during a sunny spring day.

- Goodness: Every young person that I have met in the Detention Center has a good side. There are those who have their goodness deeply buried inside and will not allow it to exist because of hopelessness and despair. Therefore, they refuse to change regardless of the love you give them. It would be great to save every child from self-destruction but we can't. However, we must try.

- See a changed man: Some of the males changed while in the Detention Center, and tried to live right when they got out. Peers, friends and families sometimes discouraged them when they made the wrong choice again. They heard words like: I told you he or she is no good. They will never be anything.

If someone kept telling me I wouldn't be anything, I probably would start believing it. We must give praises for the little changes we see in our youth and encourage them to continue with the change. We all sin and fall short of the glory of God. We must not forget the effort it took for us to change our destructive behavior.

- See my actions to prove I have changed: I know how important this is because when I was no longer being destructive, I badly wanted my wife to see I had changed but it took a tremendous amount of work. Young people must continue to work diligently by letting their actions demonstrate that they have changed regardless of negative feedback they get from others, especially their peers. Their peers can destroy them with just words or build them up with encouraging words.

- Loneliness because you are away from your family and they won't come and visit you: There are many parents who will not visit their child at the Detention Center. The youngsters have sometimes asked me to pray for their parents to come and visit them. There are kids whose parents never visited them during their stay at the Detention Center. A simple visit with love might have made a difference in the child's life. They enjoy the volunteers who reach out to them on Tuesdays and Sundays.

- See the difficulty in my life because it is hard being in the Detention Center and leaving my mother: Some of the youth want you, the reader, to know that it is not easy for them to be in the Detention Center and some are not proud of the things they've done. They really want to change but they are experiencing difficulties in controlling their attitudes and tempers. They need our prayers and support.

The last question was:
What are your feelings about getting a job?

It was very difficult for many of the youth to find a job. Many troubled youth cannot get a job. Some lack the skills to go on an interview. They don't possess the simple skills needed to complete an application. They are more likely to be involved with stealing to get some materials they need and want. They will steal before begging. Here are some of the responses I received:

- I need a job to survive.
- I need a good education to get a job.
- I need to go to school to get an education.
- If I had a job, I would not get in trouble and I would not steal or sell drugs when my parents are not rich.
- Need more jobs for teenagers. The employment age needs to be lowered to thirteen.
- Don't want a job. I am twelve years old. I just want to go to high school and graduate and go to college to get a master's degree in psychology.

When I was growing up in the south, I can't recall a time I did not have a job. There was always more work around than there were people to fill the jobs. I was not picky about my jobs. If I needed money, I went and worked various jobs such as picking cotton, sweet potatoes, harvesting melons, picking black berries and pulling tomato plants; and so did the rest of my family and friends. There was always something to keep me and the rest of the young people busy.

We need jobs and programs to keep the young people busy. They have a lot of energy, which needs to be put to constructive use.

SIX

Stopping the Destruction of Young People

What Is Destroying Our Young People?
In chapters 6 and 7, I will give more detailed information on my perspectives as to what's behind the eyes of juvenile delinquents and address some solutions. Some of my remarks will be redundant but necessary to convey my point of view. Once again, I do not claim to be an expert in adolescent psychology, but I have honestly recorded what I have personally observed, learned, and experienced.

We must not ignore how our young people are influenced by unstable families, television, movies, music, gangs, athletes, peer pressure, abuse, incest, joblessness, poverty, health, divorce, alcohol, drugs, church hypocrisy, lack of unconditional love and poor role models.

The young people of today's generation are struggling with what is right and what is wrong (and so are many adults) because of the changes in the moral val-

ues of society. Many people have turned away from the biblical values given to us by God. God's moral values and expectations have not changed from the beginning of time. For example, God's Word says:
1. You shall have no other gods before me.
2. You shall not make for yourself an idol.
3. You shall not misuse the name of the Lord, your God.
4. Remember the Sabbath day by keeping it holy.
5. Honor your father and your mother.
6. You shall not murder.
7. You shall not commit adultery.
8. You shall not steal.
9. You shall not give false testimony against your neighbor.
10. You shall not covet your neighbor's house.

Exodus 20: 3-17. We must review and discuss these commands with our children and family on a weekly basis.

During my youth, it was great to be a virgin whether male or female. It wasn't acceptable to get a woman pregnant and not marry her. The community expected you to take care of your responsibilities. But today, it is of little concern if a child is born out of wedlock.

During my youth, alcohol was the major concern, with limited access to drugs. Today, many young people use drugs and drink alcohol for comfort and to ease their pain. They also take drugs to help their pain and frustration, even though it leads to more anger and frustration. Some youngsters who are involved in alcohol and drugs have communicated that their parents gave them the drugs and alcohol. Something is absolutely wrong with that picture. Parents, as well as society are contributing to the rebellious state of our youth. Athletes who are fighting during athletic events are teaching our youth to resolve conflicts by fighting. Drug dealers are teaching youth to take an illegal shortcut to get the material things they want. Parents are getting divorced after years of marriage and they are teaching the youth to run away from commitment and responsibility.

In spite of the things that influence all young people, I believe there are two things that drive youth to criminal acts besides influences from their environment. I believe their attitudes and tempers drive their negative behavior. When you evaluate very closely what causes a young person to get into trouble, it's usually their uncontrolled attitudes and uncontrolled tempers.

Attitude is defined as a feeling or emotion toward a fact. Usually you can tell by their facial expressions, moves or positions of body that a negative attitude has developed. When a parent informs a youth, he can't hangout with a certain friend their body language will show disappointment. They will proceed to ask "why not" with a high voice. If the parent says, "Because Johnny has a bad influence on you," the negative attitude may escalate and the body language really begins to exhibit disappointment with the parent's decision. If the parent respond "Because, I am the parent," this may influence a more violent reaction or an undesirable problem. In other words, the youth's temper kicks in.

Temper means to adjust to the needs of a situation by a counterbalance. In other words, the young person will respond if you confront him or her in a negative manner. When the temper kicks in you don't perceive how the child will respond. I remember a day when my son drove his fist through the wall because he was angry with me. I also remember when he left home for three days because his attitude and temper kicked in uncontrollably. My wife and I did not prevent him from leaving since he wasn't willing to live by rules. We told him he could take his clothes but not the car we had purchased for him. With open arms, we allowed him to return provided he obeyed the rules. It was a tough decision but necessary. We look back and don't regret our decision. He is doing very well now.

In either of the above situations, a child may take an attitude which may cause his temper to kick in, which could lead to pain, frustration, destruction and anger. The greatest challenge for a parent or youth worker is to properly deal with the youth's attitude before it escalates. Unfortunately, when conflict occurs between the parent and the youth, the parent's attitude and temper take control and increase the problem. In chemistry, when you mix two incompatible substances together you are in for a big problem.

Attitude + Temper = Pain, Frustration, Anger and Destruction

When young people's negative attitudes develop, there are two key things, pain and frustration, they must control to prevent them from leading a criminal and rebellious life. When they have been hurt by a situation, an attitude of pain and frustration develops. It is essential to handle such situations in a proper manner.

Pain: When an attitude of pain occurs, the child just wants it to go away. If not properly handled or controlled, they may direct their pain to perform criminal or other undesirable acts. Their pain may have derived from a broken marriage, sexual abuse or conflict within the home or society.

Frustration: A child sometimes get an attitude of frustration because of violence in their neighborhood, with the loss of a loved one, through a drive-by shooting, or a drug related death. Youngsters are frustrated about not getting a job, pressures to perform, and the poverty that surrounds them. They are frustrated about not obtaining brand name shoes and clothes. They become frustrated when they perform poorly in school when compared to their peers. The list can go on and on.

I remember as an adult when I became frustrated about being rated average all the time on my professional job, and wanted to give up. If it wasn't for my wife's support and encouragement, I would have given up. My wife could have ignored my frustration, but I am glad God gave her the insight to intervene. We shouldn't fear to teach young people how to channel their frustrations into something positive. We cannot and should not ignore their frustration.

When the attitude of pain and frustration is not properly controlled, then the youth's temper is activated. The temper is a deadly force when not controlled. When the temper is activated, there are two uncontrollable situations that occur. The first is anger, and the second is destruction.

When youngsters become angry and lose control, they are like a raging fire and will consume everything around them unless someone intervenes with unconditional love, patience and a caring heart. A youth named Todd, became very angry with his mother, so he hit her and had no regrets. I also recall an instance where Jennifer shot her father because he was abusing her little sister. She said her anger got out of control.

I recall when my daughter was two years old and her brother did something to frustrate her. With lightning speed, she went after her brother, crawling with her mouth wide open and crying. If we had not intervened, she would have removed some skin from her brother's legs. She just sat on the floor and cried. We allowed her to cry off the frustration that had quickly turned into anger like lighting from the sky on a stormy day. She never flared up that way again. I'm glad we allowed her to sit and cry without picking her up. This is an example of how early in life a child can get an attitude and temper. No one is immune. If we can teach our children early in life about controlling their attitudes and tempers, they will have a better chance of not becoming a rebellious child.

When the attitude of pain, frustration and an angry temper is not controlled, then the temper of destruction will become the downfall of the youth. These youth become involved with various criminal acts without hesitation. They do not think of the consequences and the impact of their sins on themselves and others. They will end up in a Detention Center, county jail, or prison. Others may end up on probation, in boot camp, and foster care depending on the nature of the crime. They are very intelligent. But because of their uncontrolled attitude (pain and frustration) and temper (anger and destruction) they are becoming outcasts from society. More and more juvenile facilities are being built and expanded. The expansion and construction of more juvenile delinquent facilities is not the answer. The funds can be spent to develop family programs that address juvenile delinquents' specific problems and needs of the entire family.

A Mother's Live-in Boyfriend Impacts a Youth's Life

Here's a story about how Jerome's life was impacted negatively by his home situation because of his mother's (Debbie) live-in boyfriend and the decline of the relationship with his mother.

On March 26, 1998, Jerome, age fifteen, failed to attend a mentoring program. The program was designed to provide a mechanism by which delinquent teenagers or at-risk teens could find an end to violent and immoral behavior by encouraging a new life-style that would motivate the teens to change their destructive behavior.

Since Jerome did not attend the meeting, I called his home to verify that every thing was all right because I knew he had a problem with his attitude and temper. No one answered the telephone, so I tried several more times to reach him. I became very concerned when I couldn't reach him or any one at home to the point I started to call 911. So late Sunday night, I called and Debbie answered the phone. She shared with me that a family member in Atlanta, Georgia, had died and they went to the funeral. She sounded very despondent and said, "My boyfriend, Bob, got angry with me and left me, Joe, Lateria and Jerome in Atlanta without money and a ride home." According to Debbie, Bob was responsible for keeping the money.

Debbie said when they arrived home, Bob had broken into their house and stolen the television and other items. I asked her how Jerome was responding to the situation. She said he was very upset with Bob. I immediately became concerned about Jerome because of his temper. So I asked her if I could speak with him. She called Jerome to the telephone and told him that it was me. I asked him, "How do you feel?"

He said, "Very angry."

I said, "Jerome, don't do any thing you will regret and I will see you tomorrow." Then I asked him to please put his mother back on the telephone. She came to the telephone and told me that they didn't have any money to buy food and that she wouldn't have money until the end of the month. I told her that I was planning to drop by and see Jerome tomorrow so I could take her to the grocery store to purchase food.

I dropped by as promised and gave Debbie, Jerome, Lateria and Joe a hug. When I spoke with Jerome, I gave him some words of encouragement. I told him, "Jerome I'm proud that you didn't try to locate Bob to physically harm him. I'm proud of the progress you have made toward improving your life."

Jerome never did any thing to physically harm his mother's boyfriend. I asked Debbie what had she learned from this situation. She said, " I'm going to get out of this relationship." However, she went back into the relationship because of her love for Bob.

Jerome shared with me that he had anger toward his mother and live-in boyfriend, Bob. Jerome said, "We had a good relation until Bob came into our life. My mom and I used to be close, but now it seems like she cares more about him than me. She is always on my case."

As I was speaking with him, I could feel his pain. Yet he shared with me that he refuses to change because people want him to change. However, he does take responsibility for his own actions which means one day he will change.

I shared with him that many people knew his potential and wanted him to apply himself more. Today, Jerome is still struggling and my wife and I just keep praying for him and his family. Much of Jerome's problem is related to his home life.

He hates his true father because he abandoned them. Men need to take responsibility for their children because children need a good father for a role model if they are to become good parents themselves. I cannot comprehend the reasons why a man will produce a child and not do the best to support the mother and his child.

What Are the Solutions for Juvenile Delinquents?

Young people today need more positive role models in the church and their communities, especially their parents. How can they be taught the truth if the adults are involved in the same undesirable acts.

Half of marriages performed today end up in divorces. We are constantly sending negative messages to the youth by our actions. We must provide pre-marriage counseling if we are to reduce the divorce rate. More and more people are living together without getting married. Unmarried people are having babies. Men are marrying men, women are marrying women, and some churches are performing the ceremony. How can some churches lead when they are encouraging such acts? We must teach the youth to live by God's principles so they can have a positive influence on their peers and neighborhoods. They must be taught to control their attitudes and their tempers.

Controlled Attitude + Controlled Temper = Forgiveness, Peace, Success & Positive Self-esteem

With controlled attitudes and tempers, they can find peace, success and positive self-esteem. The Lord and society would be blessed by such accomplishment.

Who Can Make a Difference in a Troubled Youth's Life?

The Churches

Churches that are not compromising God's Word will have a profound influence on the behavior of young people and society. Discussed below are the ways churches can positively influence young people.

Churches must work together regardless of their differences in theology to assist parents in the development of parental skills.

Churches must discourage divorces and single parenting when possible.

Churches need to develop strong programs to deal with parenting skills, premarital sex, single parenting, drugs, dating, homosexuality, attitudes, tempers, finances, crime, guns and commitment. Members within the church need to live more by God's Word and let their light shine unto the world. We have many members compromising their faith because we are being selective about which sins are the worst. For God's Word says, *"Now let the fear of the Lord be upon you. Judge carefully, for with the Lord our God, there is no injustice or partiality or bribery."* 2 Chronicles 19:7.

Church members, pastors, preachers and leaders not living God-fearing lives cause many of society's problems. Churches must be different from the world yet we must live in the world.

God intended for the church to be a bright light unto the world everyday of the week and not just on Sunday. We have too many churches building within themselves instead of reaching souls outside the walls of the church. May God bless those churches that are reaching souls outside their churches and may God encourage more churches to reach out to the sinners. Each church has an excellent opportunity to reach many lost youth and families if they would just apply

God's Word daily. I believe God expects the church to reach out to those in need and in prison.

God's Word said, *"Then the King will say to those on his right, 'Come, you who are blessed by my father; take your inheritance, the kingdom prepared for you since the creation of the world. For I was hungry and you gave me something to eat. I was thirsty and you gave me something to drink. I was a stranger and you invited me in, I needed clothes and you clothed me, I was sick and you looked after me, I was in prison and you came to visit me.'"* Matthew 25:34-36

The Family

A family that prays together stays together if they are committed to each other. When a family stands strong against immoral acts together they will normally maintain a good relationship. They will less likely create a troubled youngster, but will still face problems. A strong family will grow in love and when the attitude and temper gets the best of them they will resolve the conflict. The family must have dinner together which will allow them to learn about each other's day. We can learn about our children's day around the dinner table, even if they are silent.

The family needs to spend time together outside their home such as going to the movies, bowling, traveling, walking, and studying God's Word together or just playing in the yard at home. Each family member needs personal time. We all require space to relax and meditate.

The most important investment a parent can do for their children is to give them hugs daily and tell them you love them. When parents invest hugs and love in their children's lives, their children will know how to share love with others. No matter how old they become, hugs and the words, "I love you," are the life blood of the family's heart. I call this Preventive Investment and it does not cost any thing but time.

Preventive investment is when a parent or individual spends valuable time with their family by teaching moral values, displaying physical and emotional intimacy by giving hugs, and by saying consistently I love you.

The family is the heart of society and every member of that family is attached to the heart. The family's heart has four main arteries that feed and nourish the development of the family member's characteristics. They are:

1. Physical Development
It is the family's responsibility to provide shelter, proper food, and clothing for their children. Breakfast and dinner are important meals for them to ensure they have energy to perform in school, at home or on the job.

2. Educational Development
Parents need to exercise their children's mind by reading to them when they are born until the 6th grade.

Once a child reaches the 6th grade, they probably would not like to be read to, but if they do, continue the process because it also builds relationships. It will help the youth tremendously in reading and comprehension later in life. My wife and I started reading to our children when they were infants. We read to them until they were in the sixth grade. We believe reading to them played an important role in their development.

Parents should provide tutoring for their child if needed. There is nothing wrong with saying: "I don't know the materials." Too much pride can damage or destroy the family.

3. Emotional Development

Each child and parent has an emotional need that deals with how the family will respond to love, fear, hate, and anger. The family must provide unconditional love, hugs, discipline, support, commitment, individual space, family activities that build relationships, unity, trust, respect for each other and say, *I love you,* frequently.

4. Spiritual Development

The family has a responsibility to provide the spiritual needs of the household. The father and mother should set an example for the child by studying the Bible, attending church frequently and applying the Word of God daily in their lives. A household with God-fearing parents or guardians will have a greater opportunity not to produce a troubled youth. If the family does not provide spiritual development for the youth, someone else will and the family might not like the results.

Just as the heart is a vital part of the human body so is each member of the family. When a foreign substance plugs an artery of a heart, it can damage the heart and sometimes it's fatal. Since each member of the family is attached to the heart, damage may occur when any member allows their attitude and temper to interfere with the development of a healthy family. The parent plays the most important role in the development of the family. The family must provide Preventive Investment to allow positive moral values to flow from the heart of the family, because they are one, yet distinctly different in their own way.

The family should be instrumental in assisting others in need so that their children may not become selfish. The traditional family is under attack and must fight back with the grace of God if the concept of family is to survive. The enemy knows that a family divided will have a negative impact on society. The family must become strong again in the eyesight of God. Today, I think the family's heart is badly damaged and is feeding immoral acts to the rest of the family members as well as the world. The family must use Godly principles to teach children about family, education, finance, commitment, premarital sex, drugs, homosexuality, attitude and temper and so on.

One Tuesday evening, Earl was seated in his chair in dismay in the Detention Center Gym. He said, "Rev. Strawter, my mother has awarded me to the juvenile court." Earl was trying to hold back the tears in his eyes.

I had an opportunity to spend personal time with him that day. I asked him, "How do you feel?"

He said, "I am angry, and I feel like hurting some one."

I asked him, "Why did your mother award you to the juvenile court system?"

He replied, "I gave her a difficult time."

I ask him, "Does your mother love you?"

His response was, "Yes! She never told me she didn't love me."

I told him, "Sometimes parents don't know what to do when their child becomes too rebellious. Parents sometimes seek help the best way they know how. It's not always the right way, and some parents don't care. But it appears your mother really cares for you."

Earl was encouraged to write his mother and to communicate he was sorry for being rebellious. He replied, "I told her verbally." He was strongly encouraged to write her.

I hoped Earl's mother would not totally withdraw from her son. She is the heart of his life. She can reach Earl better than the juvenile court system.

One week later, Earl said he had written his mother.

He had a big smile on his face as if he had been released from bondage. A week later, he spoke with his mother and she told him she would see him on Sunday. I wish you could have seen the smile on his face; it was as beautiful as a sunny day. He told me his mother said something she hadn't said in a long time. "I asked, "What?"

He replied "She loves me."

I advised him that he was on the right track toward change and that he must build a better relationship with his mother. Since he broke the relationship, it was his responsibility to correct the problem. He replied enthusiastically, "I will!"

I hope his mother will take the responsibility to work with her son with unconditional love. It will make a major difference in her son's life.

The family has God-given power to help rebellious youngsters. The family must exercise its rights with boldness, confidence, and commitment. We should not expect others to solve our family problems. Others can only give insight and advice but we have the responsibility to implement the changes.

The Communities

The community has a moral obligation to help families that are struggling. The society is crying for justice because so many youth are committing crime. The community is willing to pay more taxes for more prisons to be constructed but is not crying out for programs that will rehabilitate young people. The community needs to encourage programs that will teach young people how to control their attitudes and tempers (Preventive Investment). In other words, encourage society to develop programs that will mentor the troubled youth and assist them in job employment when released from a Detention Center, state or federal prisons. Money spent in these areas would be more effective long term.

When I was away from home and did something wrong during my teenage years, an adult could correct me without worrying about revenge from my parents or lawsuits. Today, most parents get offended by people who inform them that their child did something wrong or they don't want to know. Some parents will use profanity in front of their child when an adult informs them of their child's negative behavior. There are those parents who encourage their child to do wrong things, which needs to be discontinued. It takes a whole community to raise a child and that is the truth.

The Businesses

It is very difficult for juvenile delinquents to get a job because of their criminal background or behavior. A business should be made aware of their criminal acts and should not hold it against them. The business community must give them an opportunity to perform. They should be measured solely on their job performance and not past behavior.

A business that rejects a young person on the basis of a previous criminal act is lowering the individual's self-esteem. I believe businesses should take the risk and hire ex-juvenile offenders because they are investing in the future of our society and giving the youth hope for the future.

There are many companies that are more concerned about assisting students who fit their corporate image. Usually, they are not ex-juvenile offenders. Corporations need to understand that ex-juvenile delinquents are the individuals that are impacting the good students and need assistance in changing their negative behavior.

The corporations must provide "Preventive Investment" by investing funds in programs designed to reach out to potential juvenile delinquents. If corporations are not willing to invest in such job opportunities or special programs for youth, where will they go? I believe they will continue to do criminal acts if we don't give them hope and a chance to succeed.

Public School System

The public schools need to provide in-house suspension for rebellious students instead of suspending or expelling the students. In-house suspension programs should focus on the causes of the child's negative behavior.

Individuals working with the students must have the appropriate skills required to deal with the negative behavior. Then the student should be allowed back into a normal class room. When students are suspended from school frequently, they are more likely to perform an illegal act while in the streets.

The school system needs to provide smaller class rooms with no more than fifteen to twenty students per class. Smaller class rooms will allow the teachers to deal more effectively with students displaying negative behavior, therefore improving the student's academic performance and behavior.

Juvenile Court System

The court system has a responsibility to rehabilitate the young people and not act as a baby sitting service. I am convinced that programs specifically designed to deal with the issues that affect young people's attitudes and tempers such as family problems, poor performance in school, joblessness, peer pressure, lust, televisions, and gangs will make a tremendous difference in the young person's life. These programs will decrease crime and reduce the number of young people returning to the system. The family needs to be involved with the mandatory program. When young people get out of the Detention Center, many return to their same environment, which becomes a powerful struggle for them.

We need to help them change their environment by

developing programs near their neighborhoods and in their schools. It is more economical than imprisonment.

These young people need to be required to participate in programs that will help them deal with their negative behavior. I believe young people who commit murder should not be in the same Detention Center as non-murderers because of the potential impact on youngsters in the facility. A stronger program is necessary to deal with the young offenders and their parents when the families first become involved with the judicial system. I believe stronger discipline at that stage would minimize the potential of them returning to the Juvenile Detention Center. A good family program will help. For example, when drunk drivers violate the law, they are required to attend a training program. Some people feel that parents should serve time in jail for their children's criminal acts. If the parent goes to jail, who will be responsible for taking care of the remaining family members? I believe it makes more sense for the court to require the parent to attend a mandatory parenting program with the child's involvement in some aspect of the program.

When a young person is being rebellious in the Detention Center, staff workers need to identify what caused the problem without over-reacting to the situation. They should be treated as human beings regardless of their circumstances. Staff workers should never overly extend their authority toward them. When they perceive that staff is being unfair, they will band together and cause more problems. They will violate the small rules to frustrate staff and will proceed until their temper kicks in which creates major problems in terms of lockdown within the Detention Center.

When the staff confronts the youngsters, they don't like it and will try to respond back to win. Dealing with the problems as soon as possible with discussion and love can avert a youth's uncontrolled attitude and temper from being activated.

Over-reacting will only escalate the problems. Resolving the conflict with love and compassion is a great investment in preventive investment. This method requires more time versus lockup.

Many staff people of the Detention Center really care about the young people but sometimes they get tired because of being over-worked, and dealing with the daily problems encountered with juveniles. They sometimes become frustrated with them and the system. I believe every court system should hire staffs that really want to make a difference in the youths' lives and give the staffs the support they need to perform their jobs.

We need to pray for the court system because of the tremendous responsibility to rehabilitate the juvenile delinquents. We must give our support in prayer and words of encouragement. We must pray for God to give them wisdom to objectively and fairly treat the youth as the judicial system perform their duties.

Federal and State Government

The government spends billions of dollars in foreign aid, space and military programs. Yet sufficient funds are not available to:

a. Reduce the number of students in the class rooms.

b. Hire more qualified teachers.

c. Provide funding for in-house suspension for every school.

d. Provide funding for college education at a minimum cost to the students.

The government needs to allow religion back into the schools. Declining moral values have led to the downfall of many nations. Youth are very important to the present and to our future. They must know our government cares about them.

SEVEN

My Perspective of Young People

I believe as a parent that we need to be more aware of what our children are involved in and with whom they are spending their time. We should not hesitate to properly discipline our children when appropriate. According to God's Word: *"He who spares the rod hates his son, but he who loves him is careful to discipline him."* Proverbs 13:24.

We must control how we react to our children's negative behavior. We cannot properly help them with their problem if we over-react. When we react out of control, a wrong message is communicated and received by our children. We can push them further into the negative behavior that could lead to additional complications. God's Word says, *"Fathers, do not exasperate your children, instead, bring them up in the training and instruction of the Lord."* Ephesians 6:4.

When we become frustrated with our child's negative behavior, we should inform them with unconditional love of our disappointment with their negative behavior and not with them as a person. We don't want to encourage low self-esteem. We want to build children with positive self-esteem, and uplifted hearts to encourage success in the eyesight of God and the world.

There is a right time to discipline and there is a wrong time to discipline. God's Word says, *"There is a time for everything and a season for every activity under heaven."* Ecclesiastics 3:1.

Each parent must determine the appropriate time and punishment for each child because each child is different. For instance, our daughter did not like walking around the block for punishment. She thought it was stupid but it was effective. We believed in spanking and utilized it when appropriate. However, we should never be abusive to our children.

When we are abusive, we are teaching them how to become abusive. We don't want them to seek undesirable families (i.e., gangs). Everyone wants to belong to a family. We want our children to belong to a God-fearing family that cares about all people, regardless of race.

Our son enjoyed hanging out with his friends. So when his negative behavior required punishment, he could not see his friends for one to two weeks or could not make telephone calls. We had few major problems with our children but we always maintained unconditional love by hugging and telling them how important they were to us. We always insisted they attend church.

We made sure we had dinner together as often as possible and participated in most of their school activities. Their activities were a priority to us and ours were secondary. My wife made sure we had dinner together. This was important because it gave the children an opportunity to share their day.

Summary

We must all work together with the power of God to touch the life of troubled youngsters and their families. It will take the churches, businesses, communities, government and the Juvenile Courts System to help our young people to control their attitudes (pain and frustration) and tempers (anger and destruction) with specialized programs for the youth and their families. We must continue to demonstrate unconditional love and commitment to troubled youth and their families. We must stop pointing fingers because we all are responsible for touching the lives of young people and their families. We can make our streets and neighborhoods safer if we become committed to a common goal.

The goal should be to assist our young people to control their attitudes and tempers God's way. Then they will learn to wait on God to provide their needs and some of their wants. Then they will give love, respect themselves, and others, and become great citizens of this country and the world. They will produce great families in the future because of the fantastic moral values they have been taught.

A Prayer

Dear God:

You have the power and the authority to change the hearts of all people. I pray You will open the eyes of all people regarding their selfishness. Help us to turn from within and reach out to lost youth and families. Give us the strength to endure as we reach out to make a difference in an area where Satan has a stronghold. Only You can give us the strength to break the bondage of juvenile delinquency and rebellion. We need empowerment with Your wisdom, knowledge and understanding if we are to make an everlasting difference in the lives of young people and their families. I hope every church in this world will stop building within and develop an aggressive program to reach those outside the walls of the church as well as fallen Christians who have lost their way. Please show the juvenile court system and the government an alternative to imprisonment for reachable youth who are still within our grasp. Until You open their eyes, more and more prisons will be built. Lord, many are trying to find a solution to deter crime. The answer is simple and right in front of us. The answer is to put Your principles back in our churches, families, businesses, governments, schools, prisons, sports, colleges; and then You, God, will make a difference in the lives of young people, and their families in this great country, as well as the world. Please show us the way before it's too late. In Jesus' name, amen.

Your Servant,
Rev. Billy J. Strawter, Sr.

Epilogue

Thanks for taking the time to read this book. I hope your heart has been touched by God to reach troubled youth and their parents. On behalf of the juvenile delinquents and my Lord and Savior Jesus Christ, please pray for our young people. The prayer requests are listed here for you to be aware of the troubled youth concerns. I want you to become a prayer warrior for troubled youth. You have the power through prayer to make a difference.

Typical Prayer Requests

From Jackie:

Please pray for Eric so that he can see the light and get out of county jail. Pray for my sister and me. Thanks for your prayer.

Epilogue

From Lilly:

Will you please pray for me and my family? Pray specifically for my dad because I'm going to move in with him when I get out of the Juvenile Detention Center and I hardly know him. Thanks for your prayer.

From Ashley:

Pray for my Dad and my four brothers. Thanks for your prayer.

From Carol:

Could you pray for all the people in the Juvenile Detention Center to get along, to smile and never give up on doing better? Pray to God to help us all have faith and believe in ourselves.

From Sarah:

I would like for you to pray for my mother, my boy friend and everyone else in the world. Pray for my father, grandmother, and me.

From Julie:

I would like for you to please pray for me because I'm going through a difficult time. Pray that I get along with my mother. Pray for my family and my uncle.

From Linda:

Pray for my mom, dad, uncle, two-cats, sister,

brother-in-law, niece, my school, church and Pastor.

From Betty:
Please pray for my mom, my dad, brother, my boyfriend, Tom. Pray that when I get out of the Detention Center I won't be on a tether and that I will have some money when I get out and that time will fly by while I'm in the Detention Center.

From Alice:
Please pray for me so that I can get better and learn what I have done was wrong. Please pray that I get out soon and don't come back to the Detention Center.

From Susie:
Would you please pray for my family and me so it won't fall apart? Pray so I don't hurt myself. I have been thinking about killing myself, please pray for me.

From Eddie:
Please pray that I get out of the Juvenile Detention Center. Pray for my court hearing and pray that I don't return to the Detention Center.

From Thomas:
Pray that I get a job, and do well when I get out of the Detention Center.

Epilogue

From Garcia:

Please pray for my Grandmother, because she has cancer. Pray for my mother because we don't have very much. Pray that I stay out of the street and don't sell drugs or steal.

About the Author

Reverend Billy J. Strawter, Sr., is a native of Ty Ty, Georgia. He served as Associate Minister of Faith Ministries Baptist Church, Midland, Michigan. He holds a Bachelor of Science degree in Chemistry from Fort Valley State College in Georgia. He is the caring father of two young adults, Billy Jr., twenty-five, and Safiya Akilah, twenty-four. He has been married to his wife, Lee Anna, for twenty-six years.

Reverend Strawter is president and owner of EnviCare Consulting, Inc., and founder of the Omega-Alpha Club. He serves as Chaplain of the Saginaw County Juvenile Detention Center, through the Tri-County Youth for Christ as a volunteer. He serves as a member of the Saginaw County Juvenile Detention Advisory Counsel.

In 1989, Reverend Strawter was honored with the Jitsuo Morikawa Evangelism award given by the Board of National Ministries of the American Baptist

Churches. In 1979, he was named Midland's Man of the Year by the Omega Psi Phi Fraternity for outstanding community service. In 1980, he was voted one of the outstanding Men of America for Professional Achievement and Leadership Abilities. In 1997, he was awarded the Martin Luther King Community Service Award and the Rotary Vocational Service Award. His primary reason for community involvement is to offer hope to people in need. His mission is to motivate youth to make a change and succeed in society by the grace of God.